Through listening and speaking, a child's ears and mouth will be opened in the following ways:

1. As this is an interesting way of learning, children feel a greater affinity for Chinese.
2. They will naturally pick up the grammar patterns in the "dialogues".
3. They will be able to use these expressions correctly.

Try to arouse their interest in *Fun Chinese for Kids* early on, and start teaching them soon. The younger children are, the better their memory is.

Learn words through pictures, and learn conversations through recorded tapes.

▨ Pronunciation, including initials and finals, are taught using funny cartoons. Kids can quickly and easily associate these pictures with Chinese characters.

▨ The included "cassette tapes of conversations" are for centralized training for listening and speaking. Listen to the native speakers' accurate pronunciations and tones, and, just like listening to a song, you will learn with your ears first, and eventually be able to speak it out yourself.

▨ Detailed descriptions of tones, one of the most important characteristics of the Chinese language, are provided. For every tone many examples are provided for practice, which will introduce natural and accurate pronunciation into children's ears and mouths.

▨ We have listed the "rules of tones" which make pronunciation much clearer and easier to master.

▨ We also use many typical Chinese names as examples so that kids will become familiar with them.

▨ Adults who want to learn conversation-oriented instead of grammar-oriented Chinese can also begin with this textbook.

Contents

Chinese Pinyin—Initials

b	p	m	f
d	t	n	l
g	k	h	
j	q	x	
zh	ch	sh	r
z	c	s	

Chinese Pinyin—Finals

a　　o　　e　　i(yi)　　u(wu)　　ü(yu)

ai　　ei　　ao　　ou

an　　en　　ang　　eng　　er

ia(ya)　　ie(ye)　　iao(yao)　　iu(you)

ian(yan)　　in(yin)　　iang(yang)　　ing(ying)

ua(wa)　　uo(wo)　　uai(wai)　　ui(wei)

uan(wan)　　un(wen)　　uang(wang)　　ung(weng)

ong　　üe(yue)　　üan(yuan)

ün(yun)　　iong(yong)

爸 – dad
bà

天 – sky
tiān

Initials

ch

zh

m

j

k

g

l

d

n

s

h

p

t

z

x

c

r

sh

b

爸爸　bàba　(dad)

苹果　píngguǒ　(apple)

面包　miànbāo　(bread)

斧头　fǔtou　(hatchet)

Attention! "ƒ" is pronouced like "f" in English.

蛋糕　dàngāo　(cake)

糖 táng (candy)

鸟 niǎo (bird)

鹿 lù (deer)

狗 gǒu (dog)

Attention! "G,k,h" are all pronounced with a sound in the throat.

可乐 kělè (Coke)

喝　hē (drink)

姐姐　jiějie (sister)

Attention! "J,q,x" are pronounced with the tip of the tongue behind the lower teeth.

汽车　qìchē (car)

西瓜　xīguā (watermelon)

纸 zhǐ (paper)

"Zh,ch,sh,r" are pronounced with the tip of the tongue raised and curled back, as if there were a sweet on the tongue.

叉子 chāzi (fork)

狮子 shīzi (lion)

人 rén (people)

字 zì (character)

Attention! The tongue should be behind the lower teeth when pronouncing "z, s, c".

草莓 cǎoméi (strawberry)

蒜 suàn (garlic)

Finals

ch

ai

ang

wai   k

yi

ao   wu   en   yang   ei

an   yin

yao   ye   wan   ya   ti

eng   er

阿姨 āyí (aunt)

噢 ō (oh)

饿 è (hungry)

笔 bǐ (pen)

Attention! When there is no initial preceding "i,u" they are written in the following manner: i → yi, u → wu, ü → yu. When "i" follows "zh,ch,sh, r,z,c,s", it is pronounced lightly.

一 yī (one)

路 lù (road)

雾 wù (fog)

旅游 lǚyóu (travel)

雨 yǔ (rain)

彩虹 cǎihóng (rainbow)

累 lèi (tired)

猫 māo (cat)

猴子 hóuzi (monkey)

山 shān (mountain)

门 mén (door)

脏 zāng (dirty)

冷 lěng (cold)

儿子 érzi (son)

Attention! "Er" is pronounced like "r" in English with a raised tongue.

牙膏 yágāo (toothpaste)

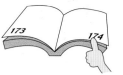

页 yè (page)

19

药 yào (medicine)

加油 jiāyóu (come on)

眼睛 yǎnjing (eye)

饮料 yǐnliào (drink)

羊 yáng (sheep)

电影 diànyǐng (film)

娃娃 wáwa (doll)

我 wǒ (I)

外貌 wàimào (appearance)

喂 wèi (Hello)

玩 wán (play)

问题 wèntí (question)

王 wáng (king)

瓮 wèng (jar)

痛 tòng (painful)

ong

月亮 yuèliang (moon)

yue

院子 yuànzi (yard)

yuan

拳头 quántou (fist)

üan

云彩 yúncai (cloud)

裙子 qúnzi (skirt)

Attention! When "j, q, x" are followed by "ü", the two small dots will be omitted.

勇士 yǒngshì (soldier)

Tones

What are tones?

So different tones represent different meanings?

Of course! mā means mother and mǎ means horse. The syllable ma is the same, but the tone is different.

How do we mark the tones?

We place tone markers above the following five vowels in order of priority: a, o, e, i, u. For example, if a syllable contains an a, it is marked hǎo. If there is no a, but there is an o, then it is marked zuò, if there is neither a nor o, then the e is marked xiè, if it has i and/or u, the tone mark should be over the second one, as in liù, shuì. When marking i, the dot should be omitted, as in qī.

I see. So how are these tones pronounced?

Well, try doing the tone exercises on the next page. Listen to the tapes and practice, and you should have no trouble at all learning it.

The 1st tone

Attention: The first tone is the "so" sound of the seven basic musical tones. It is high and level.

风 fēng (wind)

猪 zhū (pig)

高 gāo (high)

花 huā (flower)

书 shū (book)

声音 shēngyīn (sound)

乌鸦 wūyā (crow)

Attention: The second tone starts in the mid-range and then rises.

谜 mí (riddle)

龙 lóng (dragon)

您 nín (you)

学习 xuéxí (study)

邮局 yóujú (post office)

黎明 límíng (dawn)

钱 qián (money)

Attention: This tone first falls towards the lower registers, and then rises again.

手 shǒu (hand)

水 shuǐ (water)

你 nǐ (you)

雨 yǔ (rain)

脸 liǎn (face)

土 tǔ (earth)

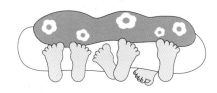

脚 jiǎo (foot)

Attention: This is a falling sound, like the word "Hey!" spoken in a short, forceful tone.

剑 jiàn (sword)

路 lù (road)

梦 mèng (dream)

热 rè (hot)

病 bìng (sick)

问号 wènhào

(question mark)

再见 zàijiàn (goodbye)

The light tone

Attention: This is pronounced quickly and lightly. It is not marked.

衣服 yīfu (clothes)

爷爷 yéye (grandpa)

影子 yǐngzi (shadow)

朋友 péngyou (friend)

枕头 zhěntou (pillow)

学生 xuésheng (student)

知识 zhīshi (knowledge)

What does changing tone mean?

If a character is difficult to pronounce in its original tone because of the other characters around it, the tone of the previous character will be changed accordingly. This is called changing tone. Look at the following explanations and exercises, and you will soon understand.

Rules of tone changes:

1. ∨(3rd tone) + ∨(3rd tone) ➡ /(2nd tone) + ∨(3rd tone)

2. ∨(3rd tone) + —(1st tone), /(2nd tone), \(4th tone), (light tone)
   ➡∨(half 3rd tone) + —(1st tone), /(2nd tone), \(4th tone), (light tone)

Attention: A half third tone is pronounced only as the falling part, the rising part being omitted.

3. —(yī), 不(bù) + \(4th tone) ➡ —(yí), 不(bú) + \(4th tone)

4. —(yī) + —(1st tone), /(2nd tone), ∨(3rd tone) ➡ —(yì) \(4th tone)

Attention: Characters with changing tones will be marked with their original tones, but the characters — and 不 can be marked with their changed tones.

33

Tone changes of the 3rd tone

3rd tone(v) + 3rd tone(v) ➡ 2nd tone(/) + 3rd tone(v)

水果 shuǐguǒ (fruit) 粉笔 fěnbǐ (chalk) 雨伞 yǔsǎn (umbrella)

3rd tone (v) + 1st tone(—) ➡ half 3rd tone(v) + 1st tone(—)
2nd tone(/)   2nd tone(/)
4th tone(\)   4th tone(\)
light tone   light tone

老师 lǎoshī (teacher)

彩虹 cǎihóng (rainbow)

考试 kǎoshì (exam)

耳朵 ěrduo (ear)

yī(—)+4th tone(\) ➜ yí(/) + 4th tone(\)

一半 yíbàn (a half)　一块 yíkuài (a piece)　一样 yíyàng (the same)

一(yī)+1st tone(–) ➜ yì(\)+1st tone(–)
　　　2nd tone(/)　　　　2nd tone(/)
　　　3rd tone(v)　　　　3rd tone(v)

一天 yìtiān (a day)

一家 yìjiā (a family)

一年 yìnián (a year)

一百 yìbǎi (a hundred)

Tone changes of 不(bù)

不(bù)+ 4th tone (\) ➔ 不(bú)+ 4th tone(\)

不是 búshì (no)

不用 búyòng (not use)

不看 búkàn (not look)

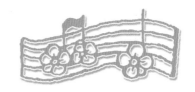

shēng rì kuài lè
生日快乐
Happy Birthday to You

Zhù nǐ shēngrì kuàilè
祝你生日快乐，
Happy birthday to you,

Zhù nǐ shēngrì kuàilè
祝你生日快乐，
Happy birthday to you,

Zhù nǐ shēngrì kuàilè
祝你生日快乐，
Happy birthday to you,

Zhù nǐ shēngrì kuàilè
祝你生日快乐。
Happy birthday to you.

生日快乐

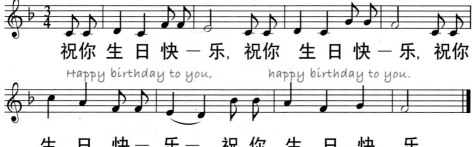

祝你 生 日 快 — 乐，祝你 生 日 快 — 乐，祝你
Happy birthday to you, happy birthday to you.

生 日 快 — 乐 —，祝 你 生 日 快 乐。
Happy birthday to you, happy birthday to you.

37

石头剪刀布
Rock, Scissors, Cloth

① 石头剪刀布!
Rock,scissors, cloth!

② 再一次!
Again!

③ 赢了!
I won!

④ 输了!
I lost!

shí tou jiǎn dāo bù
① 石头剪刀布!
Rock, scissors, cloth!

zài yí cì
② 再一次!
Again!

yíng le
③ 赢了!
I won!

shū le
④ 输了!
I lost!

石头 shítou (rock)   剪刀 jiǎndāo (scissors)   布 bù (cloth)

开始吧！

Let's Begin!

① 早。
Morning.

② 你好。
How do you do?

③ 晚上好
Good evening.

④ 再见
Goodbye.

zǎo
① 早。
Morning.

wǎn shang hǎo
③ 晚上好。
Good evening.

nǐ hǎo
② 你好。
How do you do?

zài jiàn
④ 再见。
Goodbye.

① 谢谢。
Thank you.

② 对不起。
I am sorry.

③ 开始了。
Begin.

④ 吃饱了。
I am full.

xiè xie
① 谢谢。
Thank you.

duì bu qǐ
② 对不起。
I am sorry.

kāi shǐ le
③ 开始了。
Begin.

chī bǎo le
④ 吃饱了。
I am full.

① 站起来吧！
Stand up.

② 坐下吧！
Sit down.

③ 念吧！
Let's read.

④ 写吧！
Let's write.

⑤ 唱吧！
Let's sing.

zhàn qǐ lái ba
① 站起来吧！
Stand up.

zuò xia ba
② 坐下吧！
Sit down.

niàn ba
③ 念吧！
Let's read.

xiě ba
④ 写吧！
Let's write.

chàng ba
⑤ 唱吧！
Let's sing.

在哪里?

1 珊珊, 你的鞋子在哪里?

2 在这里。

3 毛毛, 你的伞在哪里?

4 在那里。

5 明明, 你的学校在哪里?

6 在那里。

7 我家也在那里。

Where is it?

what are they saying

shān shan   nǐ de xié zi zài nǎ li
① 珊珊，你的鞋子在哪里？
Shanshan, where are your shoes?

zài zhè li
② 在这里。
They are here.

máo mao   nǐ de sǎn zài nǎ li
③ 毛毛，你的伞在哪里？
Maomao, where is your umbralla?

zài nà li
④ 在那里。
It's there.

míng ming   nǐ de xué xiào zài nǎ li
⑤ 明明，你的学校在哪里？
Mingming, where is your school?

zài nà li
⑥ 在那里。
It's over there.

wǒ jiā yě zài nà li
⑦ 我家也在那里。
My house is over there too.

这是谁的?

① 这是谁的书?

② 这是我的（书）。

③ 那是谁的书包?

④ 那是我的书包。

⑤ 这是谁的?

⑥ 冬冬的照相机。

⑦ 珊珊的帽子。

⑧ 明明的妈妈的鞋子。

Whose is it?

what are they saying

1
zhè shì shéi de shū
这是谁的书？
Whose book is this?

2
zhè shì wǒ de shū
这是我的（书）。
It's my book.

3
nà shì shéi de shū bāo
那是谁的书包？
Whose bag is that?

4
nà shì wǒ de shū bāo
那是我的书包。
That's my bag.

5
zhè shì shéi de
这是谁的？
Whose is it?

6
dōng dong de zhào xiàng jī
冬冬的照相机。
Dongdong's camera.

7
shān shan de mào zi
珊珊的帽子。
Shanshan's hat.

8
míng ming de mā ma de xié zi
明明的妈妈的鞋子。
Mingming's mother's shoes.

那不是我的

That's not mine

what are they saying

❶ zhè shì měi líng de qiān bǐ ma
这是美灵的铅笔吗?
Is this Meiling's pencil?

❷ bú shì bú shì wǒ de
不是，不是我的。
No, it isn't. It is not mine.

❸ nà shì shéi de
那，是谁的?
Then, whose is it?

❹ nà shì tiān yòu de
那是天佑的。
It's Tianyou's

❺ zhè shì niú niú de shū ma
这是牛牛的书吗?
Is this Niuniu's book?

❻ bù bú shì
不，不是。
No, it isn't.

❼ nà shì shéi de
那，是谁的?
Then, whose is it?

❽ nà shì dà nián de
那是大年的。
It's Danian's.

那个孩子是谁？

Who is that kid?

 what are they saying

①
zhè ge hái zi shì shéi
这个孩子是谁？
Who is this kid?

②
zhè ge hái zi shì dòu dou
这个孩子是豆豆。
This is Doudou.

③
nà ge hái zi shì shéi
那个孩子是谁？
Who is that kid?

④
nà ge hái zi shì máo mao
那个孩子是毛毛。
That is Maomao.

⑤
nà ge hái zi ne
那个孩子呢？
Who is that kid?

⑥
nà ge hái zi shì tíng ting
那个孩子是婷婷。
That is Tingting.

喜欢吗？讨厌吗？

豆豆，
① 你喜欢学校吗？

② 嗯！喜欢！非常喜欢！

③ 佳佳，你喜欢蛇吗？

④ 不，讨厌！非常讨厌。

Do you like it or hate it?

what are they saying

① dòu dou   nǐ xǐ huan xué xiào ma

豆豆，你喜欢学校吗？

Doudou, do you like school?

② ng   xǐ huan   fēi cháng xǐ huan

嗯！喜欢！非常喜欢！

Well, yes. I like it very much.

③ jiā jia   nǐ xǐ huan shé ma

佳佳，你喜欢蛇吗？

Jiajia, do you like snakes?

④ bù   tǎo yàn   fēi cháng tǎo yàn

不，讨厌！非常讨厌。

No, I don't. I hate them very much.

LEARN SOME WORDS STEP BY STEP

桃子 táozi (peach)

可乐 kělè (Coke)

小狗 xiǎogǒu (dog)

蛋糕 dàngāo (cake)

老鼠 lǎoshǔ (mouse)

妈妈 māma (mum)

打针 dǎ zhēn (inject)

旅游 lǚyóu (travel)

数目

1	一 yī (one)
2	二 èr (two)
3	三 sān (three)
4	四 sì (four)
5	五 wǔ (five)
6	六 liù (six)
7	七 qī (seven)
8	八 bā (eight)
9	九 jiǔ (nine)
10	十 shí (ten)

11	十一 shíyī (eleven)
12	十二 shí'èr (twelve)
13	十三 shísān (thirteen)
14	十四 shísì (fourteen)
15	十五 shíwǔ (fifteen)
16	十六 shíliù (sixteen)
17	十七 shíqī (seventeen)
18	十八 shíbā (eighteen)
19	十九 shíjiǔ (nineteen)
20	二十 èrshí (twenty)

Numbers

30	三十 sānshí (thirty)		700	七百 qībǎi (seven hundred)
40	四十 sìshí (forty)		800	八百 bābǎi (eight hundred)
50	五十 wǔshí (fifty)		900	九百 jiǔbǎi (nine hundreds)
60	六十 liùshí (sixty)		1000	一千 yìqiān (a thousand)
70	七十 qīshí (seventy)		2000	二(两)千 èr(liǎng)qiān (two thousand)
80	八十 bāshí (eighty)		3000	三千 sānqiān (three thousand)
90	九十 jiǔshí (ninety)		4000	四千 sìqiān (four thousand)
100	一百 yìbǎi (a hundred)		5000	五千 wǔqiān (five thousand)
200	二百 èrbǎi (two hundred)		6000	六千 liùqiān (six thousand)
300	三百 sānbǎi (three hundred)		7000	七千 qīqiān (seven thousand)
400	四百 sìbǎi (four hundred)		8000	八千 bāqiān (eight thousand)
500	五百 wǔbǎi (five hundred)		9000	九千 jiǔqiān (nine thousand)
600	六百 liùbǎi (six hundred)		10000	一万 yíwàn (ten thousand)

多少钱?

中国的货币 (zhōngguó de huòbì) Chinese currency (called Renminbi)

100 元 (元 yuan is also called 块 kuai.)

50 元

10 元

5 元

2 元

1 元

5 角 (角 jiao is also called 毛 mao.)

2 角

1 角

How much is it?

what are they saying

xiāng jiāo duō shao qián
① 香蕉多少钱？
How much is the banana?

èr bǎi yuán
② 200 元。
Two hundred yuan.

píng guǒ duō shao qián
③ 苹果多少钱？
How much is the apple?

yìbǎiwǔshí yuán
④ 150 元。
One hundred and fifty yuan

LEARN SOME WORDS STEP BY STEP

 西瓜 xīguā (watermelon)

 甜瓜 tiánguā (melon)

 香蕉 xiāngjiāo (banana)

5元5角 wǔ yuán wǔ jiǎo   15元 shí wǔ yuán   10元 shí yuán

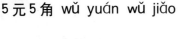 橘子 júzi (orange)

 桃子 táozi (peach)

12元 shí'èr yuán   12元 shí'èr yuán

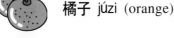 葡萄 pútao (grape)

 苹果 píngguǒ (apple)

6元 liù yuán   6元 liù yuán

63

11

几月?

sān yuè
三月
(March)

sì yuè
四月
(April)

wǔ yuè
五月
(May)

chūn tiān
春天
(Spring)

liù yuè
六月
(June)

qī yuè
七月
(July)

bā yuè
八月
(August)

xià tiān
夏天
(Summer)

jiǔ yuè
九月
(September)

shí yuè
十月
(October)

shí yī yuè
十一月
(November)

qiū tiān
秋天
(Autumn)

shí'èr yuè
十二月
(December)

yī yuè
一月
(January)

èr yuè
二月
(February)

dōng tiān
冬天
(Winter)

Which month is it?

 what are they saying

jǐ yuè
①几月？
Which month is it?

sān yuè
②三月。
March.

xià ge yuè jǐ yuè
③下个月几月？
Which month is next?

sì yuè
④四月。
April.

65

几号?

一号 yī hào (1st)	十三号 shísān hào (13th)
二号 èr hào (2nd)	十四号 shísì hào (14th)
三号 sān hào (3rd)	十五号 shíwǔ hào (15th)
四号 sì hào (4th)	十六号 shíliù hào (16th)
五号 wǔ hào (5th)	十七号 shíqī hào (17th)
六号 liù hào (6th)	十八号 shíbā hào (18th)
七号 qī hào (7th)	十九号 shíjiǔ hào (19th)
八号 bā hào (8th)	二十号 èrshí hào (20th)
九号 jiǔ hào (9th)	二十四号 èrshísì hào (24th)
十号 shí hào (10th)	二十七号 èrshíqī hào (27th)
十一号 shíyī hào (11th)	二十八号 èrshíbā hào (28th)
十二号 shí'èr hào (12th)	二十九号 èrshíjiǔ hào (29th)

What is the date today?

① 今天几号?
What is the date today?

② 5号。
5th.

③ 明天几号?
What will be the date tomorrow?

④ 6号。
6th.

what are they saying

jīn tiān jǐ hào
① 今天几号?
What is the date today?

wǔ hào
② 5号。
5th.

míng tiān jǐ hào
③ 明天几号?
What will be the date tomorrow?

liù hào
④ 6号。
6th.

nǐ shǔ shén me

你属什么？

What is your symbolic animal?

老鼠 lǎoshǔ (rat)　　　　牛 niú (ox)　　　　虎 hǔ (tiger)

兔 tù (hare)　　　　龙 lóng (dragon)　　　　蛇 shé (snake)

马 mǎ (horse)　　　　羊 yáng (sheep)　　　　猴子 hóuzi (monkey)

鸡 jī (cock)　　　　狗 gǒu (dog)　　　　猪 zhū (hog)

xiǎo xīng xīng

小星星

Little Star

yì shǎn yì shǎn liàng jīng jīng
一闪一闪亮晶晶，

Twinkle, twinkle, little star,

mǎn tiān dōu shì xiǎo xīng xīng
满天都是小星星，

How I wonder what you are,

guà zài tiān shàng fàng guāng míng
挂在天上放光明，

Up above the world so high,

hǎo xiàng xǔ duō xiǎo yǎn jīng
好像许多小眼睛，

Like a diamond in the sky,

yì shǎn yì shǎn liàng jīng jīng
一闪一闪亮晶晶，

Twinkle, twinkle, little star,

mǎn tiān dōu shì xiǎo xīng xīng
满天都是小星星。

How I wonder what you are.

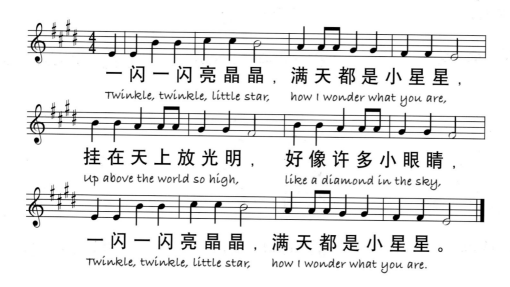

一闪一闪亮晶晶，满天都是小星星，
Twinkle, twinkle, little star, *how I wonder what you are,*

挂在天上放光明，好像许多小眼睛，
Up above the world so high, *like a diamond in the sky,*

一闪一闪亮晶晶，满天都是小星星。
Twinkle, twinkle, little star, *how I wonder what you are.*

69

星期几?

xīng qī yī
星期一
Monday

xīng qī èr
星期二
Tuesday

xīng qī sān
星期三
Wednesday

xīng qī sì
星期四
Thursday

xīng qī wǔ
星期五
Friday

xīng qī liù
星期六
Saturday

xīng qī rì
星期日
Sunday

zuótiān
昨天
yesterday

jīn tiān
今天
today

míngtiān
明天
tomorrow

What day is today?

what are they saying

jīn tiān xīng qī jǐ
①今天星期几?
What day is today?

xīng qī liù
②星期六。
Saturday.

nà míng tiān xīng qī jǐ
③那，明天星期几?
What day will be tomorrow?

xīng qī tiān xué xiào fàng jià
④星期天。学校放假!
Sunday . On Sundays school will be closed.

几点?

yì diǎn
一点
one o'clock

liǎng diǎn
两点
two o'clock

sān diǎn
三点
three o'clock

sì diǎn
四点
four o'clock

wǔ diǎn
五点
five o'clock

liù diǎn
六点
six o'clock

qī diǎn
七点
seven o'clock

bā diǎn
八点
eight o'clock

jiǔ diǎn
九点
nine o'clock

shí diǎn
十点
ten o'clock

shí yī diǎn
十一点
eleven o'clock

shí èr diǎn
十二点
twelve o'clock

What time is it?

① 现在几点？
What time is it now?

② 现在是六点。
It's six.

what are they saying

    xiàn zài jǐ diǎn
① 现在几点？
What time is it now?

    xiàn zài shì liù diǎn
② 现在是六点。
It's six.

几分?

yì fēn
1分
one minute

èr fēn
2分
two minutes

sān fēn
3分
three minutes

sì fēn
4分
four minutes

wǔ fēn
5分
five minutes

liù fēn
6分
six minutes

qī fēn
7分
seven minutes

bā fēn
8分
eight minutes

jiǔ fēn
9分
nine minutes

shí fēn
10分
ten minutes

shíyī fēn
11分
eleven minutes

shí'èr fēn
12分
twelve minutes

LEARN SOME WORDS STEP BY STEP

yì diǎn yì fēn
1:01
one past one

sān diǎn wǔ fēn
3:05
five past three

sān diǎn bàn
3:30
half past three

sì diǎn shí fēn
4:10
ten past four

sì diǎn èrshíbā fēn
4:28
twenty-eight past four

bā diǎn sānshiwǔ fēn
8:35
thirty-five past eight

① 现在几点？
What time is it now?

② 现在是 1点10分。
It's ten past one.

③ 现在几点？
What time is it now?

④ 现在是 9点30分。
It's half past nine.

Nihao

what are they saying

① xiàn zài jǐ diǎn
现在几点？
What time is it now?

② xàn zài shì yì diǎn shí fēn
现在是 1 点 10 分。
It's ten past one.

③ xiàn zài jǐ diǎn
现在几点？
What time is it now?

④ xiàn zài shì jiǔ diǎn sānshí fēn
现在是 9 点 30 分。
It's half past nine.

LEARN SOME WORDS STEP BY STEP

jiǔ diǎn wǔshí fēn
9 : 50
nine fifty

shíyī diǎn shíbā fēn
11 : 18
eighteen past eleven

shí'èr diǎn shísān fēn
12 : 13
thirteen past twelve

liù diǎn sìshíwǔ fēn
6 : 45
six forty-five

qī diǎn qī fēn
7 : 07
seven past seven

shí'èr diǎn jiǔ fēn
12 : 09
nine past twelve

热吗？

Is it hot?

what are they saying

① jīn tiān rè ma
今天热吗?
Is it hot today?

② ǹg rè a
嗯，热啊!
Yes, it is.

③ wǒ bú rè
我不热。
I am not hot.

④ jīn tiān lěng ma
今天冷吗?
Is it cold today?

⑤ ǹg lěng
嗯，冷。
Yes, it is.

⑥ wǒ bù lěng
我不冷。
I am not cold.

⑦ dōng dong nǐ shēn tǐ chà mà
冬冬，你身体差吗?
Dongdong, do you have bad health?

⑧ bù wǒ hěn qiáng zhuàng
不，我很强 壮。
No, I don't. I am very healthy.

长吗?

(1)

Is it long?

what are they saying

① dà xiàng de bí zi cháng ma
大象的鼻子长吗？
Is the elephant's tusk long?

② ǹg hěn cháng
嗯，很长。
Yes. It is very long.

③ nà dà xiàng de wěi ba yě cháng ma
那，大象的尾巴也长吗？
Then, is the elephant's tail long, too?

④ bù hěn duǎn
不，很短。
No. It is very short.

⑤ nǐ mā ma xiōng ma
你妈妈凶吗？
Is your mother strict to you?

⑥ ǹg hěn xiōng
嗯，很凶。
Yes, she is.

⑦ nà nǐ bà ba ne
那，你爸爸呢？
What about your father?

⑧ hěn hé ǎi
很和蔼。
He is very gentle.

(2)

① 天空是蓝色的吗?

② 嗯,是蓝色的。

③ 那,云呢?

④ 云是白的。

⑤ 香蕉是什么颜色呢?

⑥ 黄色的。

 **what are they saying**

1 tiān kōng shì lán sè de ma
天空是蓝色的吗?
Is the sky blue?

2 ǹg   shì lán sè de
嗯，是蓝色的。
Yes, it is.

3 nà   yún ne
那，云呢?
What about the clouds?

4 yún shì   bái de
云是白的。
They are white.

5 xiāng jiāo shì shén me yán sè ne
香蕉是什么颜色呢?
What color are bananas?

6 huáng sè de
黄色的。
They are yellow.

Contents for Volume II

Appendices

It is so interesting to learn Chinese! I will try my best to learn the second volume!

Appendices

❶ 家族 jiāzú (Family Members)

爷爷 yéye (grandfather)

奶奶 nǎinai (grandmother)

爸爸 bàba (father)

妈妈 māma (mother)

哥哥 gēge
(elder brother)

姐姐 jiějie
(elder sister)

我 wǒ
(me)

妹妹 mèimei
(younger sister)

弟弟 dìdi
(younger brother)

② 水果 shuǐguǒ (Fruits)

苹果 píngguǒ
(apple)

梨子 lízi
(pear)

橘子 júzi
(orange)

柿子 shìzi
(persimmon)

西瓜 xīguā
(watermelon)

葡萄 pútao
(grape)

草莓 cǎoméi
(strawberry)

桃子 táozi
(peach)

香蕉 xiāngjiāo
(banana)

番茄 fānqié
(tomato)

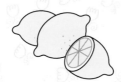

柠檬 níngméng
(lemon)

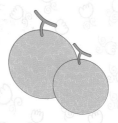

甜瓜 tiánguā
(melon)

❸ 蔬菜 shūcài (Vegetables)

白菜 báicài
(Chinese cabbage)

萝卜 luóbo
(radish)

葱 cōng
(green Chinese onion)

洋葱 yángcōng
(onion)

胡萝卜 húluóbo
(carrot)

黄瓜 huánggua
(cucumber)

菠菜 bōcài
(spinach)

茄子 qiézi
(eggplant)

大蒜 dàsuàn
(garlic)

南瓜 nánguā
(pumpkin)

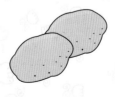

马铃薯 mǎlíngshǔ
(potato)

洋白菜 yángbáicài
(cabbage)

4 动物 dòngwù (Animals)

狮子 shīzi

(lion)

鳄鱼 èyú

(crocodile)

鹿 lù

(deer)

大象 dàxiàng

(elephant)

熊 xióng

(bear)

长颈鹿 chángjǐnglù

(giraffe)

山羊 shānyáng

(goat)

蛇 shé

(snake)

河马 hémǎ

(hippopotamus)

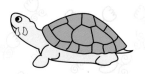

乌龟 wūguī

(tortoise)

骆驼 luòtuo

(camel)

狐狸 húli

(fox)

❺ 鸟 niǎo (Birds)

麻雀 máquè
(sparrow)

燕子 yànzi
(swallow)

鸽子 gēzi
(pigeon)

雁 yàn
(wild goose)

乌鸦 wūyā
(crow)

猫头鹰 māotóuyīng
(owl)

鹦鹉 yīngwǔ
(parrot)

鸭子 yāzi
(duck)

秃鹫 tūjiù
(condor)

鹤 hè
(crane)

海鸥 hǎi'ōu
(seagull)

野鸡 yějī
(pheasant)

6 文具 wénjù (Stationery)

铅笔 qiānbǐ
(pencil)

钢笔 gāngbǐ
(pen)

本子 běnzi
(notebook)

纸 zhǐ
(paper)

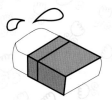

橡皮 xiàngpí
(eraser)

胶水 jiāoshuǐ
(glue)

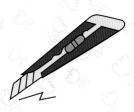

小刀 xiǎodāo
(knife)

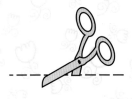

剪刀 jiǎndāo
(scissors)

尺子 chǐzi
(ruler)

透明胶带 tòumíng jiāodài
(adhesive tape)

修正液 xiūzhèngyè
(correction fluid)

图钉 túdīng
(thumbtack)

7 电器 diànqì (Electrical Appliances)

电脑 diànnǎo
(computer)

电视机 diànshìjī
(television set)

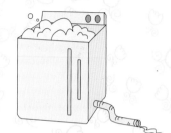

洗衣机 xǐyījī
(washing machine)

冰箱 bīngxiāng
(refrigerator)

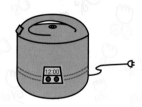

电锅 diànguō
(electric rice cooker)

电熨斗 diànyùndou
(electric iron)

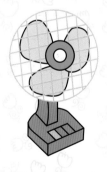

电扇 diànshàn
(electric fan)

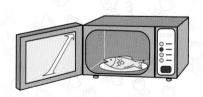

微波炉 wēibōlú
(microwave oven)

照相机 zhàoxiàngjī
(camera)

8 乐器 yuèqì (Musical Instruments)

钢琴 gāngqín

(piano)

吉他 jítā

(guitar)

小提琴 xiǎotíqín

(violin)

口琴 kǒuqín

(harmonica)

大提琴 dàtíqín

(cello)

长笛 chángdí

(flute)

风琴 fēngqín

(organ)

喇叭 lǎba

(trumpet)

琴 qín

(stringed instrument)

鼓 gǔ

(drum)

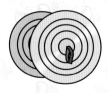

铙钹 náobó

(cymbals)

笛子 dízi

(pipes)

图书在版编目(CIP)数据

快乐儿童汉语.1 ／ SISA 汉语文化苑编著. - 北京:
华语教学出版社，2004.1
ISBN 7-80052-927-4

I. 快... Ⅱ.S... Ⅲ. 汉语－儿童教育－对外汉语教学－教材 Ⅳ.H195.4

中国版本图书馆 CIP 数据核字(2003)第 090000 号

韩国时事出版社授权华语教学出版社在中国独家出版发行汉英版

Fun Chinese for Kids

快乐儿童汉语 ①

编著:SISA 汉语文化苑

英文翻译: 韩芙云   英文编辑: 韩 晖
中文编辑: 贾寅淮   印刷监制: 佟汉东
装帧设计: 唐少文

©华语教学出版社
华语教学出版社出版
（中国北京百万庄路 24 号）
邮政编码 100037
电话: 010-68995871
传真: 010-68326333
网址：www. sinolingua.com.cn
电子信箱: hyjx@sinolingua.com.cn
河北省大厂回族自治县彩虹印刷有限公司印刷
中国国际图书贸易总公司海外发行
（中国北京车公庄西路 35 号）
北京邮政信箱第 399 号 邮政编码 100044
新华书店国内发行
2004 年（16 开）第一版
2006 年第二次印刷
（汉英）
著作权合同登记图字 01-2002-5415
ISBN 7 - 80052 - 927 - 4 / H · 1512(外)
9 – CE – 3592PA
定价：38.00 元

ALLISON

Fun Chinese for Kids

Mother and child can study together

快乐儿童汉语

Compiled by SISA Chinese Culture Center

1

FOREWORD

First, teach children to speak .
Learning Chinese will become easy.

Learn how to speak first

As people become more and more interested in the Chinese language, the number of Chinese learners is increasing fast. However, it is always difficult to make up one's mind to start learning Chinese, and even those who start often give up later. If asked the reason why, they usually say: "It is too difficult to pronounce."

Chinese is a "tonal" language, which means that a single syllable can be pronounced at different pitches, and syllables of different pitches have different meanings. For this reason most people find the Chinese language difficult to learn. Therefore it is important to study pronunciation and tones first. If you learn accurate pronunciation and tones, you will have a basic command of Chinese.

Children who know nothing about grammar can learn a foreign language faster than adults. That's because they simply imitate what they hear, and remember "the language itself" rather than memorizing complicated rules of grammar. Therefore, beginning with correct pronunciation and tones is a shortcut for children to learn the rest of the language.

First of all, you must "open" a child's ears and mouth

People who have been studying a foreign language for a long time often do not speak well when meeting foreigners, simply because they focus too much on grammar and words.

This textbook is designed using dialogues applicable to children's everyday life. While studying this textbook, you can listen to the accompanying cassette tapes to hear dialogues between native speakers. Practicing and reciting these dialogues will lead a child's ears and mouth to "open" naturally.